THE CLEVELAND BROWNS

Published by Creative Education, Inc., 123 South Broad Street, Mankato, Minnesota 56001

Copyright © 1986 by Creative Education, Inc. International copyrights reserved in all countries. No part of this book may be reproduced in any form without written permission from the publisher. Printed in the United States.

Library of Congress Catalog Card No.: 85-72611

ISBN: 0-88682-029-4

SOUTHWEST LIBRARY
PRATT, KANSAS

THE CLEVELAND BROWNS

JAMES R. ROTHAUS

CREATIVE EDUCATION

CLEVELAND BROWNS

Sunday, January 11, 1981. The air was so cold in Ohio that the soda vendors at Cleveland Stadium had to serve frozen pop to the fans. The weather man pegged the temperature at zero. The north wind howled in off Lake Erie, cutting through heavy clothing like a frigid knife.

Despite the numbing cold, nearly 78,000 fans turned out to watch the Cleveland Browns battle the Raiders in a do-or-die playoff battle. It was the Browns' first playoff appearance in nine years, and no north wind could keep the anxious Cleveland fans at home.

As the players tromped onto the field for warm-ups that day, they could feel the icy air bite into their lungs. The frozen playing surface looked like whitish-green concrete. As the running backs practiced their cuts, they slipped helplessly to the ground.

That was on the outside. On the inside, the Browns were smiling. They knew the weather would work in their favor. After all, since 1945, Cleveland football teams had hammered their way through season after season of bitter winters. The Cleveland tradition was wrapped in a mantle of cold, gray days, but it was warmed by the memories of many great victories. The Browns hoped to deepen that tradition with one more victory today.

Out on the field, Cleveland's brilliant little quarterback, Brian Sipe, was working the stiffness out of his throw-

Did you know?

The 1950 title game between the Browns and the Giants was a strange one. Played in near-zero temperatures, the game became a kicking duel and ended with the peculiar score of 8-3 in favor of Cleveland.

Coach Paul Brown (left) was ruthless in his pursuit of smart, strong football players. He found one of the greatest players in NFL history when he drafted Otto Graham (right).

> **Did you know?**
>
> *A stroke of "bad luck" brought the great Jim Brown to Cleveland in 1957. The Browns had intended to draft a quarterback first that year, but two coin flips went against them. Drawing sixth in the draft, they had to "settle" for a legend in the making.*

ing arm. With field conditions at their worst, Sipe knew he'd be moving the ball through the air. Though receivers Dave Logan and Ozzie Newsome were wearing gloves, Sipe's rocket-like spirals slapped their outstretched fingers like a snapping ruler.

Up in the stands, the fans huddled against the cold in layers of cozy coats, knitted nose-warmers and thick wool socks. The NFL game they were about to witness would be the second coldest playoff game since the Dallas-Green Bay deep freeze in 1967. Only one thought took the chill off the fans: If they could defeat the Raiders today, the Cleveland Browns would then be one small step away from football's final contest—the Super Bowl!

From the opening kickoff, it was obvious that Lady Luck would play a big part in the game. Bobbled passes, bumbled hand-offs and squibbed kicks filled the frozen afternoon as both teams struggled up and down the slippery playing field. The Browns fumbled six times but somehow rolled out of the pile-ups with five recoveries. Sipe had three passes picked off—one by safety Mike Davis and two by Lester "Mr. Stickum" Hayes.

Late in the first quarter, cornerback Ron Bolton finally broke a scoreless tie when he intercepted a Jim Plunkett pass and darted 42 yards for a TD. With an early 6-0 lead, the Cleveland fans had a good excuse to stomp their chilly feet.

But the Raiders had come to play. In the second quarter, Mark van Eeghen capped off a 64-yard drive by plunging into paydirt from the one-yard line. The scoreboard told the story. At halftime the Browns were down, 7-6.

Clearing the path for Motley was stocky guard Bill Willis. Both players were later named to the Hall of Fame.

Deep in the Cleveland locker room, head coach Sam Rutigliano was a man on fire. His face was a brilliant shade of red. His eyes were ablaze as he reminded his team of the Cleveland tradition. "Hold on, men," he would tell them. "Hold on, and grind it out."

Something in Rutigliano's voice fanned the embers of the Cleveland offense. When they hit the field in the third quarter, they cut through the Oakland line like a laser through empty space.

The two Pruitts (Mike and Greg) took turns scrambling around the ends. Then, changing pace, one or the other would cut up the Raiders' middle, darting past the claws of big Dave Browning or "Mad Stork" Ted Hendricks. When two drives stalled in the third period, placekicker Don Cockroft booted two perfect field goals of 30 and 29 yards to give the bad-news Browns the lead, 12-7.

In the fourth quarter, the Raiders blasted their way back. In a bone-jarring 80-yard drive, Plunkett marched his team down the frozen turf. Short passes to Don Chandler and teeth-rattling runs by van Eeghen pushed a touchdown past the Cleveland defense. With Oakland back on top, 14-12, the fourth quarter now promised to be an uphill battle for the Browns.

As evening eerily came down around the field, the Browns gathered themselves together for one last charge at the stubborn Raiders. With the offense blasting Oakland off the line of scrimmage, Cleveland steadily advanced the ball up the field. Sipe was brilliant; the Pruitts were awesome; and the fans were exploding in a frenzy of frantic cheering. But time was running out.

Sipe moved his team to the Raiders' 13-yard-line.

Did you know?

Larry "Bobo" Braziel, Cleveland's lean, mean cornerback, is a vegetarian.

During his long and glorious career, Otto Graham led the Browns to an unheard-of seven professional championships. (1954)

> **Did you know?**
>
> *At 15, Art Modell dropped out of high school and cleaned hulls in a Brooklyn shipyard to help his financially-strapped family after the death of his father. Twenty years later, Art was able to purchase the Cleveland Browns for $4 million!*

Then, with only 49 seconds showing on the clock, he called for time-out. Rutigliano paced the sidelines. He had a terrible decision to make. He knew a short field goal would win the game, but the frozen ball and gusty head wind made the kick a chancy one. Finally, Rutigliano instructed Sipe to try a pass to Logan. If Logan was covered, Sipe was to hurl the ball all the way to Lake Erie.

A pass! Though caught off guard by the unusual call, Oakland swarmed the Browns' receivers. Logan was covered, but Sipe spotted Ozzie "Wizard of Oz" Newsome in the end zone. Sipe tried a desperation pass, but the football fluttered as it left his hand. Newsome and Oakland's Mike Davis leaped for the ball together. But it was too late for the Browns as Davis gathered the ball to his burly chest.

Cleveland had lost. There would be no Super Bowl for the Browns, but the players would later say that this cold, bitter, disappointing game would launch this team into the Eighties with a renewed sense of the old Cleveland spirit. This game had made them look back. It had made them remember the good old days—the days when the Browns were always in the running for No. 1.

THE TEAM THAT WAS NAMED AFTER ITS COACH

In 1945, a wealthy Cleveland businessman named Arthur (Mickey) McBride heard a rumor that another professional football league was being formed. As a kid, McBride had grown up in Chicago selling newspapers on the corner. He had learned to love the town of Cleveland. Now he saw a chance to do something for the people. With no one backing him up, McBride bought the football franchise with his own money.

This wasn't the first time there had been pro football in Cleveland. There had been a professional club in the city during the 1920's. That team had been called the Panthers, but somehow it had never been very popular.

Mickey McBride wasn't about to let this new Cleveland team fail. He wanted a head coach who was good and tough—one who would run the team with a strong hand. He didn't look too far before he found Paul Brown.

Brown was the kind of guy who always meant what he said and did what he promised. An intense and demanding young man, he had started his coaching career in his hometown at mighty Massillon (Ohio) High School. After leading Massillon to six state championships, Brown was invited to coach Ohio State University. After only one year, the Buckeyes clinched the 1942 National Championship. A few months later, when World War II got hot, Brown insisted on registering for the draft. Ohio State said good-bye to its coach.

During the war, Brown stayed sharp by coaching at Great Lakes Military Academy. It was here that Mickey McBride finally caught up with him. The two men liked each other. After brief talks, it was announced that Brown would coach Cleveland's entry into the All-America Football Conference (AAFC). His salary would be about $20,000 a year—a big bundle of money in those days. At 38, Brown had become the highest-paid coach in the nation!

The first thing the team needed was a nickname.

Did you know?

His real name is William Banks, but years ago his sister nicknamed him Chip. "When you start listing the gifts a player needs to be a great linebacker," said Cleveland coach Sam Rutigliano, "you end up describing what Chip Banks has."

Paul Brown, flanked by Ray Renfro (left) and Chuck Noll and Billy Reynolds, gazes intently at the gridiron action during a 1953 contest against the old Chicago Cardinals.

McBride held a "name that team" contest in Cleveland. First prize would be a $1,000 war bond. Thirty-six entrants chose the name "Panthers" because of the old pro team, but Paul Brown said no.

"I want no part of that name," he told newspapers. "That old Panther team failed. I won't start out with anything that smacks of failure."

A large number of entrants suggested the team be named the "Browns" after their coach. Brown really didn't care for that idea, either, but he finally gave in, and the team became known as the Cleveland Browns. That made Brown the only man in pro football history to ever have a team named after him. Orange, brown (of course) and white were selected as team colors.

The next great task was to assemble a strong, capable team. That challenge was right up Paul Brown's alley.

Did you know?

As of the 1984 season, five Cleveland uniforms had been retired out of respect to the players who had worn the following numbers for the Browns: 14 (Otto Graham); 32 (Jim Brown); 45 (Ernie Davis); 46 (Don Fleming); and 76 (Lou Groza).

OTTO GRAHAM COMES TO TOWN

Paul Brown remains one of the true legends of professional football. Though he spoke in a quiet voice, it was never difficult to hear him.

"You were afraid to breathe while he was talking," said one Cleveland veteran. "Coach Brown was not a big man, but he could make big men shiver just by looking at them."

Brown had strict rules for his players. He demanded "gentlemanly" behavior — or else!

Sportswriter Ray Didinger ("The Professionals") made a copy of a typical Paul Brown speech. It went like this:

> **Did you know?**
>
> *Mike Baab, the enormous (6-4, 270-pound) Cleveland center was the 115th player selected in the 1982 draft, but he quickly proved that he was a diamond in the rough. One of the strongest players in the league, Baab is credited with paving the way for Mike Pruitt's fourth—and most spectacular—1,000-yard season!*

"We don't want any butchers on this team. Don't eat with your elbows on the table and don't make noise when you eat." (This was training camp, the first day!) "We intend to have good people on this football team because that's the kind who win the big ones.

"If you are a drinker, you weaken the team and we don't want you. We're here for just one thing — to win.

"You must watch how you dress, your language and the company you keep. When we're on the road, stay away from the stranger who may want to talk to you in the hotel lobby. Maybe he isn't a gambler, but stay from him anyway."

Though many top collegiate players were frightened off by Brown's tough-minded rules, others were strongly attracted to his grit and honesty.

One such college standout was hard-charging tailback Otto Graham. Blessed with a sturdy 6'1", 195-pound body, Graham liked to "plot" his way up the field, slipping and faking a path through even the craftiest tacklers. Here was a player who could run...who could think... who could lead. Slowly an idea took shape in the back of Coach Brown's mind. He would invite Graham to play for Cleveland under one condition—that he become a quarterback. The rest is history.

Quarterback Otto Graham would go on to lead the Browns to 10-straight championship games, earning a reputation as the finest T-formation quarterback of all time. But he did it in sound company.

Brown filled out the rest of the roster with a special blend of players, most of whom had played for him at Ohio State and Great Lakes. There was Lou (The Toe) Groza, Dante Lavelli, Mac Speedie and Ed (Special

The championship line-up, (left to right) End Dante Lavelli, Center Frank Gatski, Coach Brown, QB Otto Graham and tackle/kicker Lou Groza pose for a group shot the day before they whipped the Rams 38-14 to claim the '55 NFL title.

> **Did you know?**
>
> *Doug English of the Detroit Lions had this to say about Cincinnati center Mike Baab: "Mike is as strong as nine acres of Texas onions!"*

Delivery) Jones—just to name a few. Brown also did something that no pro coach had ever done before—he actively recruited black players to join his team. Two in particular—Marion Motley and Bill Willis—went on to incredible careers at Cleveland. When their playing days were over, both were inducted into the Pro Football Hall of Fame!

THE LATE 1940's— UNFORGETTABLE!

The Browns opened their very first season in 1946 by thrashing the Miami Seahawks, 44-0, at Cleveland Stadium. Paul Brown's hard-nosed discipline had paid off. His team ran through their plays like a well-tuned—but always unpredictable—machine.

First, Motley might charge around right end. Next, Willis might slam up the middle, carrying tacklers with him as he went. Then, just when the defense had contained the run, Graham might fade back and hurl a perfect spiral into the arms of tricky Dante Lavelli.

Leaving chaos in their wake, the Browns racked up seven straight victories that first season. In the process, they outscored their hapless opponents 180 to 34. Naturally, when the Browns played at home, Cleveland fans jammed into cavernous Cleveland Stadium, cheering wildly.

By season's end, the mighty Browns had tallied an impressive 12-2 record—but they weren't through yet! In the first title playoff, before 41,181 fans at Cleveland, the Browns came from behind twice to defeat the New York Yankees and claim the AFC crown.

The very next year, 1947, the Browns pranced, danced and slashed their way to a 12-1-1 season. Perhaps the most exciting game was the famous 28-28 tie with New York. In that game, New York came out charging and ran up a 28-0 lead on the bewildered Browns. But Cleveland was not about to be embarrassed by the city boys from New York. They came back clawing and hissing like wounded cats. When the final gun sounded, the game was deadlocked. More than 70,000 New York fans showed their appreciation by jumping to their feet to applaud both weary teams.

In the AAFC title game that year, the two teams met again, but this time Otto Graham and Marion Motley took the Yankees apart in front of their hometown fans. Even grim-faced Coach Brown was able to crack a championship smile—his second in two years.

Then came the 1948 season which old-timers still recall as one of the most exciting seasons ever for the Browns. In the off-season, Coach Brown had beefed up his offense by trading for halfback Dub Jones, as well as linemen Alex Agase and Forrest (Chubby) Gregg. Even though premier receiver Dante Lavelli was out until mid-season with a broken leg, the team went on a 19-game winning tear. During that streak, the team racked up their first perfect season and their third straight AAFC title, but the best was yet to come.

In the title game, the Browns so outclassed the Buffalo Bills that the Cleveland bench-warmers were playing in the regulars' slots early in the fourth period. Fullback Motley so devastated Buffalo with his punishing running style, that he himself out-gained the entire Bills' team, 133 yards to 63!

Did you know?

How important is an NFL field goal kicker? During the 1983 season, Cleveland's Matt Bahr received four game balls from his teammates for his clutch game-winning performances!

> **Did you know?**
>
> *Local boy makes good: Linebacker Tom "Cooz" Cousineau, achieved his own triple crown: A local athlete who gained high school All-America honors, then advanced to collegiate stardom for state team and finally to a pro career for hometown team.*

The year 1949 was to be the final season for the old All-America Football Conference. Just two days before the end of the season, it was announced that the league had merged with the NFL. Oddly enough, the success of the Browns had actually contributed to the failure of the league. Explained Coach Brown: "We were too good, if that sounds possible. In Cleveland the fans stopped coming to our games because they just assumed we'd go out and dominate the opposition so strongly, there would be no contest."

During the 1949 season, for example, the Browns piled up a 9-1-2 record (including a 61-14 destruction of Los Angeles) and outscored their opponents almost two to one. In the L.A. game, Graham threw for six touchdown passes, four of which went to—you guessed it—Mr. Lavelli.

The Browns met the 49ers in the last AAFC title game, but with only 22,550 fans looking on. They routed the 49ers, 21-7, to win their fourth consecutive league championship. Believe it! The record shows that the Cleveland Browns were the only team ever to win an AAFC title!

THE BROWNS JOIN THE NFL

You can be sure that the rest of the teams in the NFL had heard all about the Browns' domination of the AAFC. Still, the NFL players weren't impressed. They figured the Browns would fall apart in the "big leagues."

During the off-season, Coach Brown swapped players

Two high-flying Philadelphia Eagles weren't enough to stop Dante Lavelli (56) from hauling in another of Otto Graham's long bombs. (1951)

Lou "The Toe" Groza specialized in long-distance field goals during the 20 years he was a Brown.(1950)

around to different teams in the league so he could tighten up his defense. Rex Bumgardner and John Kissell came from the Bills, and Cleveland drafted big John Sandusky to plug up the middle of the line.

In the season opener, 71,237 Philadelphia Eagles fans swarmed to the stadium to watch their NFL Championship team take on the "wimpy" newcomers from the AAFC. Surprise! For four straight quarters the Browns manhandled the Eagles in every phase of the game. When the clock touched zero, the Browns pranced off the gridiron with a convincing 35-10 victory in the bag. No doubt about it—Cleveland had shown the entire NFL that they were for real.

The rest of the 1950 season fell into the classic Browns' pattern. Graham to Lavelli for six. Motley up the middle for 14. Bill Willis on the end sweep for 46 yards and the touchdown. After 14 games, the Browns had a 12-2 record. They headed into a playoff game against their arch-rivals, the New York Giants. And what a game it turned out to be!

In 10-degree weather at Cleveland, it was the golden toe of Lou Groza that had built up a slim fourth-quarter margin for the Browns. Though New York almost rallied late in the fourth period, Willis, in a one-man defensive surge, dropped New York's Eugene (Choo Choo) Roberts from behind at the Browns' 4-yard-line. Game over!

Paul Brown had been a professional football coach for five seasons. Already he had led his team to the league title five times!

Did you know?

Early start: Even when he was in grade school, Cleveland punter Steve Cox dreamed of becoming an NFL kicker. As a youth, Steve was a six-time regional Punt, Pass and Kick winner (ages 8-13) and twice a national finalist!

> **Did you know?**
>
> *Here's how fullback Johnny "B-1" Davis explains his nickname: "I like to block. I don't consider it a good one unless I knock the other guy down. I guess that's why they call me B-1. They say it's like dropping a bomb."*

A TURNING POINT

The following year the Browns opened their season with a loss to the 49ers in San Francisco, 24-10. Coach Brown was so angry about his players' performance that he scared them right back into the winning column. From then on, the Browns rolled to 11 straight victories and a title game showdown with the Los Angeles Rams.

It was there that Paul Brown experienced an odd turning point in his career. In the title game, played beneath sunny southern California skies, Rams quarterback Norm Van Brocklin—a future Hall of Famer—broke a deadlocked game when he pitched to Tom Fears, who rambled 73 yards for the score. The fourth quarter ended with the Rams on top, 24-17. For the first time in years, Paul Brown had tasted defeat in the most important game of the season. It was a sign of things to come.

The following year, 1952, the Browns were challenged by Philadelphia and New York but still managed to win their third straight Eastern Conference title.

In the championship game, however, Bobby Layne led the Detroit Lions to a convincing victory. Though the Browns moved deep into Lion territory several times, the mighty Lion defense always held them away from the goal line. In the third period, Detroit's shifty Doak Walker streaked 67 yards for a touchdown. That score went unanswered the rest of the day. The final showed the Lions on top, 17-7.

In 1953 David Jones bought the Browns from McBride for $600,000. McBride had no way of knowing that six years later the team would be sold again for more than six times that amount—$3,925,000!

The decision was made to keep Brown on as head coach of the 1953 team. Brown responded to the new owner's vote of confidence by arranging a series of sly trades and draft picks to strengthen the team. When the season opened, the Browns bolted to 11 victories in a row, including a 62-14 drubbing of the New York Giants before 40,000 delighted hometown fans.

In the NFL Championship game, the Browns met Detroit for the second straight year. Field goals were traded back and forth, keeping the two teams neck-and-neck until late in the game. Then, with only 4:10 remaining, Layne stepped back and heaved a long TD pass to Jim Doran. Once again, the Browns had lost the most important game of the season by the smallest of margins—17-16. It was a heart-breaking loss for the entire Cleveland organization.

At the end of that season, several of the original Cleveland workhorses hung up their cleats and retired. Coach Brown busied himself, looking high and low for quality players to replace those dependable old warriors. Fred (Curly) Morrison filled the backfield gap left when Willis retired. Maurie Bassett (who was billed as the next Marion Motley) and Chet Hanulak were picked up from the college ranks.

Struggling with new players, the 1954 team started off with a disappointing 1-2 record, but they built up steam and raced through the rest of the schedule with only one more loss. Strangely, for the third year in a row, the Browns met the Lions in the NFL Championship game. Unlike the previous two years, however, the outcome of this contest would be totally different.

Did you know?

Versatile tackle Doug Dieken is the only player in Browns' history to recover a fumble, score a TD, block a punt, score a safety, gain a first down and return a kickoff.

Cleveland's legendary Otto Graham—the grand old quarterback—was spectacular in the title game, which was played the day after Christmas, 1954. Otto completed nine of 12 passes for 163 yards and three touchdowns. Then he bootlegged his way into the end zone three more times to make the final tally, Browns 56, Lions 10. It was the first time Cleveland had beaten Detroit in seven meetings. More important, it was the first time the Browns had claimed the NFL Championship since its first year in the league.

Did you know?

Team comic Doug Dieken says he knows exactly how people will remember his career: "Holding penalty, number 73."

OTTO GRAHAM "ALMOST" RETIRES

At the end of the 1954 season, Graham retired from the team. Four games into the 1955 campaign, however, it was obvious the Cleveland magic was lacking without him, so Coach Brown tried to coax him back. Graham couldn't say no.

Laboring with old injuries, the 34-year-old Graham rallied his team and once again led them into the NFL title game. This time the Browns would play Los Angeles in California.

A record crowd of over 87,000 fans turned up to see the Rams wage war with the Browns. Graham wasted no time. He completed 14 of 25 passes for 209 yards and two TD's—and carried the ball himself for two more scores. It was an all-Cleveland day as the Browns picked off a total of six passes from the ravaged Rams.

Late in the game, Paul Brown called Otto Graham out of what would be his last NFL game. Even though the

People will still say that there was never a football player like the immortal Jim Brown. (1960)

> **Did you know?**
>
> *Cornerback Hanford Dixon was asked to describe the important qualities necessary to play his position. "Well, you have to have a short memory," he grinned. "If I'm beat, I'll learn from it, forget it and go from there."*

Rams' fans had booed him at the beginning of the game, they now rose to their feet for a two-minute standing ovation. There were tears in Graham's eyes as he trotted to the sidelines for the final time.

By winning that game, 38-14, the Browns had become two-time NFL champs. Statistics revealed that each year Graham had played for the Browns, the team had been involved in the title game. Over his ten-year career, Otto had led the team to seven professional football championships—a feat no other quarterback has ever come close to matching. He had thrown for over 13,000 yards during his career and tossed 88 touchdown passes.

In 1965, by vote of the football writers of America, Otto Graham's jersey was enshrined in the Pro Football Hall of Fame.

THE GREATEST RUNNING BACK OF ALL TIME?

In 1956, the Browns limped through the season without Graham, Lavelli and Dub Jones, finishing with a puny 5-7 record. It was the first time in the team's 10-year history that it had failed to enter post-season play.

Prior to the 1957 season, Coach Brown shopped around the college ranks, searching for a quarterback to replace Graham. On the way, he discovered a young running back by the name of James Nathaniel Brown.

Perhaps no running back has ever been better equipped to play fullback than Jim Brown. He stood

Burly Lyle Alzado, one of the rare breed who could control the tempo of an entire game. Alzado later jumped ship to join the L.A. Raiders.

6'2" and weighed a strapping 228 pounds. His glistening, apple-butter-brown skin was stretched over great slabs of rippling muscle. Standing still, Brown looked like a finely polished bronze statue. And when he ran toward the end zone, he streaked across the ground like an animal in pursuit of prey.

Even in his rookie season, Brown was a one-man terror. Entire defenses keyed on him. The big, burly linemen knew that Cleveland QB Milt Plum would hand off to Brown an average of 20 times per game—and they vowed to stop him. Brown was gang-tackled. He was jabbed with elbows. He was illegally slugged and bashed. But he seldom lost his temper. Jim Brown let his running be his revenge.

In his first season, he rambled for a league-leading 942 yards and nine touchdowns. The Browns made the playoffs, but the high-flying Detroit Lions whipped them in the final game, 50-14. Even so, Brown was the unanaimous choice for NFL Rookie of the Year.

It was no fluke. From the first play of the following year—1958—Jim Brown broke loose and never looked back. The Browns jumped off to a 5-0 start, and there was talk of an undefeated season in the air. Then disaster struck. Coach Brown was forced to bench QB Bobby Mitchell in favor of Leroy Bolden.

Though the Browns pulled together behind their new quarterback—and actually had a good shot at the playoffs— their hopes went down the drain when wily Tom Landry, the coach of the Giants, figured a way to shut Brown down for one key game. Still, when the final tallies for the 1958 season were posted, Brown had rushed for an astounding 1,527 yards!

> **Did you know?**
>
> *When Cleveland defensive end Elvis Franks was 9 years old, a fire destroyed his family's home. Elvis' clothes caught fire and he was hospitalized for nine months. Today, he regularly visits the kids at Cleveland Clinic's childrens ward, cheering on their efforts at recovery.*

Battling Brian Sipe emerged as the NFL's finest all-around quarterback in 1979. His record 3,793 yards passing shattered the legendary Otto Graham's all-time record.

> **Did you know?**
>
> *Big Bob Golic on playing nose tackle: "To play nose tackle, you have to be unemployed or crazy. I was unemployed. The other part is still up in the air...Nobody interviews nose tackles. They don't think we can talk."*

The legend grew. Year in and year out, Brown could always find a way to rip off huge chunks of yardage. Though the rest of the coaches in the league studied through the night to figure out ways to stop him, Brown plowed right through their plans. He seemed indestructible! Through 118 straight games with Cleveland, only once did Jimmy Brown leave the field with an injury. There was only one problem. Despite Brown's superhuman performances, Cleveland couldn't seem to win the NFL Championship.

The fans grew restless as their team struggled through seasons of 9-3, 7-5, 8-3-1, 8-5-1, 7-6-1. To make matters worse, tension was building between Coach Brown and fullback Brown. Their personalities clashed, and this put a strain on the entire team. Finally, with the poor showing in the 1962 season, Cleveland's new owner, Art Modell, called Paul Brown into his office. Modell looked his proud coach squarely in the eyes and told him he was fired.

After 17 years as the only coach of the team that had been named after him, the great Paul Brown packed up his 158-48-8 record, along with eight league championships and retired from pro football. He would remain in retirement until 1968 when he would take over the coaching duties of the new team in Ohio—the Cincinnati Bengals.

Meanwhile, with Paul Brown off his mind, Jim Brown ran wild in 1963. When the wounded defenders had all been removed from the field, the record showed that Brown had crashed his way for 1,863 yards and 15 touchdowns. That record would not be broken until ten years later when a young man named O.J. Simpson

At 6'7" and 280 pounds, offensive tackle Cody Risien commanded the New York Jets' attention in 1985 action.

Did you know?

Mighty Mite: Just 5-7 and 165 pounds, little Dino Hall set nine club records (one NFL record) in his role as a kickoff and punt returner for the Browns! He has always been his teams' smallest player, including pee wee football at age seven!

would rush for 2,003 yards in a single season.

With Brown out in front again in 1964, Cleveland rolled to a 10-3-1 regular-season record. They brushed off the New York Giants, 52-20, in a playoff game, and then got set to meet the Baltimore Colts for the NFL Championship. Though the experts were betting on the Colts, Jim Brown had other ideas. This was his chance to win the NFL title—a goal that had evaded the great running back all his career.

Two days after Christmas, Jim Brown drove the hometown crowd into a frenzy by pounding his way past the bewildered Colts for 114 yards. Up in the stands, the Cleveland fans, decked out in orange and black, chanted "Jimmy, Jimmy, Jimmy." When the final gun sounded, the Browns left the field in triumph. It was Jim Brown's finest moment in professional football.

And then came strange news. Less than one year later, after Cleveland lost to the Green Bay Packers in a playoff game on a snow-covered field in Wisconsin, Jim Brown suddenly retired from pro football at the height of his career.

The newspaper and television reporters were puzzled. Modell and Coach Blanton Collier were shocked. Why had Jim Brown made such an unusual decision? He was still the most potent offensive weapon in the game. He was only 30-years-old. He was in perfect health. Why?

Jim Brown's answer was simple. He calmly told reporters that the football phase of his life was over. No second thoughts. No regrets. He had simply decided to devote his time to other interests. Football was fine, but other things were important, too. He would let his record stand on its own. And what a record it was!

THE UP AND DOWN YEARS

After Brown left Cleveland, the team experienced several years of roller coaster rides. They'd rise to the top of the league, only to plummet in the playoffs.

In 1966, Cleveland lost to Dallas in a bid for the Browns' third straight Eastern Division title. The next year, Cleveland faced Dallas again for a spot in the NFL Championship game, but the brilliant pass-catching of Cowboy speedster Bob Hayes downed the Browns, 52-14.

Coach Blanton Collier retired in 1970 and his spot was taken by Nick Skorich. Skorich lasted only three seasons before he was replaced by Forrest Gregg. Gregg stayed less than one season before he, too, was fired. Finally, after a long and careful search, the Browns found Sam Rutigliano.

THE BROWNS BOUNCE BACK

When Coach Rutigliano arrived in Cleveland, he rocked the team out of its sleep and started a serious rebuilding policy. He made several key trades, including the acquisition of a wild and wooly defensive machine by the name of Lyle Alzado.

Rutigliano came right out and told the fans to get ready for a comeback in Cleveland. Instantly, he delivered.

The very first year, Rutigliano steered the Browns to an 8-8 record—its best in five years. The next year, 1979, he guided the Browns to a 9-7 season. Seven of

Did you know?

In college, Eddie Johnson's teammates nicknamed him, "Georgia Assassin" because he shaved his head at the start of each season, and then tackled like a man possessed.

> **Did you know?**
>
> *Linebacker Clay Matthews says he just loves to blitz: "To me, a sack by a linebacker or defensive lineman means the same as a touchdown for a back or a receiver."*

those nine wins were pulled out in the fourth quarter or overtime. Because of their heart-stopping finishes, the Browns' entitled their highlight film for 1979, "The Kardiac Kids."

In 1980, the Pruitts—Mike and Greg (no relation)—rallied back from nagging injuries to spark a reckless and daring offensive style. Brian Sipe and Ozzie Newsome teamed up to form one of the most dangerous passing threats in the NFL. Sipe, who had his best year to date as a pro, threw for over 4,000 yards and 30 touchdowns. Mike Pruitt rambled for over 1,000 yards and six TD's.

Charles White, the 1980 Heisman Trophy winner, also joined the Browns' potent backfield as Rutigliano sought to add more power and punch to his lineup. The strategy worked. White bulled his way for five touchdowns in his rookie season.

On defense, burly Lyle Alzado continued to close off the ends with a bone-breaking style of attack. Clay Matthews and All-Pro safety Thom Darden tightened the loose reins of the defense, too. No doubt about it, something special was brewing in Cleveland.

That something was pride. There was pride in the fact that the Cleveland Browns were on the road to another NFL Championship. Pride in the fact that players and fans were caught up in "Cleveland Fever." And most of all, pride for Rutigliano and the Browns because once again they were bringing home victories to the proud people who live on the shores of Lake Erie. The Cleveland Browns—the team that once sought nothing less than championships for its fans—were getting ready to do it again.

Safety Don Rogers, shown here in his 1984 rookie season, breathed new life into the Cleveland defense.

Mike Pruitt (42) churns toward daylight as Calvin Hill prepares to lower the boom on Washington Redskin Pete Wysocki (50).

RETURN TO THE TOP

In 1980, the Browns came back to clinch the AFC Central Division title for the first time in nine years. Then, on an icy, mid-winter day the Cleveland players and nearly 80,000 of their fans came together to take on the bullies from the West Coast—the big, bad Oakland Raiders.

The Raiders' defense knew all about Sipe and Pruitt, and they weren't about to be dazzled by their big-play offense. Four times Sipe marched the Browns deep into Oakland territory, and each time the Raiders held.

Veteran kicker Don Cockroft booted four gorgeous field goals for Cleveland, but it was not enough. Oakland's Jim Plunkett put two touchdowns on the board, and the Browns went down, 14-12.

That particular loss seemed to poke a permanent hole in the Cleveland balloon. A deflated feeling was evident at next year's training camp, and the feeling spilled over into regular-season play. Inconsistency was the rule in '81. One week the defense would come apart; the next week it would hold, but the offense would bog down. Cleveland ended the season 5-11, and Rutigliano fumed.

"That's it," he snapped. "This summer we're cleaning house."

THE BIG BUILD-UP

Actually, Rutigliano didn't just clean house—he practically built a new one. First, Alzado was traded to the

> **Did you know?**
>
> *For years, Cleveland quarterback Paul McDonald spearheaded a group called "Paul's Pals," an activities group for kids with cancer, leukemia and other blood disorders at Cleveland's Rainbow Babies and Children's Hospital.*

> **Did you know?**
>
> *Watch out for Ozzie! Coach Sam Rutigliano paid tight end Ozzie Newsome the highest compliment: "There isn't a receiver in football who catches in traffic the way Ozzie does. He's gonna break every record that was ever written by this club."*

Raiders. Next, running backs Greg Pruitt and Calvin Hill got their walking papers. Filling those holes wouldn't be easy, but Rutigliano found some help in the Browns' own backyard.

For starters, there was gritty Ohio native Tom Cousineau. As a youngster, Tom had grown up in Lakewood, Ohio, and he had spent many Sunday afternoons in the stands of Cleveland Stadium, rooting for the Browns. He had played his college ball at Ohio State, earning All-America linebacker honors in the bargain. He was drafted by the Buffalo Bills, but rather than play there, he signed with Montreal of the Canadian Football League. Despite instant stardom in Montreal, Cousineau wanted to come home...to Cleveland. Rutigliano was only too happy to sign him.

"All we need now is a big-play man on defense," figured Rutigliano. "We need a guy who can make the big hit, who can pop the ball loose in those close games for us."

Out in California there was just such a player. His name was Chip Banks, and he played for USC. "He turns game films into horror films for the other team," said one astonished scout. "Banks should be renamed 'Tanks.' That's how he hits—like a tank."

That's just what Rutigliano wanted to hear. He made Banks the Browns' first choice in the college draft. In later rounds, Cleveland picked defensive end Keith Baldwin and center Mike Baab. Both would become starters along with Banks and Cousineau.

It took a couple weeks to work out the kinks, but soon Cleveland was running like a well-oiled machine. Even so, it required a gutsy late-season charge, led by

Oh, Ozzie! Newsome hauls in another rainbow in 1984.

> **Did you know?**
>
> Ironman! Despite all those bruising tackles, rugged fullback Mike Pruitt just keeps on chugging. Over a six-year period Mike missed only one game because of injury!

back-up quarterback Paul McDonald, to land the Browns in the playoffs. Not even a season-ending 27-10 loss to the Raiders could spoil the new sense of spirit that was spreading throughout the club.

"We may be a couple years away," smiled Rutigliano, "but we're back on the winning track—that's for sure."

How true! With wiry little Brian Sipe back at the helm in 1983, Cleveland's offense exploded. Sipe's favorite target was Ozzie Newsome who now emerged as one of football's premier receivers. The big, fast tight-end simply could not be covered with one man. And when Newsome got the ball, it usually took two or three tacklers to drag the big guy down.

If Newsome was tough, Banks was tougher. "Chip Banks is one of those guys who hates to lose," said the coach. "He has no respect for pain, and he's virtually fearless. I know I wouldn't want to be on the receiving end of his tackles."

True to form, Banks almost single-handedly destroyed New England. He returned an interception for a 65-yard touchdown. He recorded two sacks, knocked down two passes and made six solo tackles in the 30-0 win over the Pats.

Sipe, who desperately wanted a Super Bowl in his final season with the Browns, played brilliantly through the closing weeks. But in the final regular-season game it was the hard-charging Seattle Seahawks who narrowly edged the Browns out of the playoffs. Cleveland's 9-7 record was good, but not quite good enough. It was back to the drawing board for '84.

All during the off-season, the sounds of clanging weights rang loud and clear in the Cleveland exercise facility. If hard work is the path to victory, reasoned the Browns, no one will work harder than we will.

With each passing day their spirit and their conviction grew brighter and firmer. By the end of summer, the Browns were pawing the ground in anticipation. For the first time since the Jim Brown days, they were united in their belief that they could take on—and beat—the best in the league.

"This is the most outstanding team we have had in ten years," said club owner Art Modell. Rutigliano agreed with his boss. "I would say that we are the favorites to win the Central Division," said the coach. The reporters around the country agreed. Almost everyone said this would be the Browns' year.

One reason for all the optimism was Cleveland's new quarterback, Paul McDonald. He had taken the Browns to the playoffs as a substitute in 1982. Now he was ready to go one step farther.

"It's like a fantasy come true," said McDonald. "I've been able to watch Brian Sipe, one of the league's best, for the past four seasons. Now I'm the starter and I'm ready for the next chapter. This team is primed to write its own ticket to the Super Bowl."

Football, of course, is a strange game. The trophy does not always go to the best team or the best players. What starts off as a dream for a great team can easily turn to a nightmare with a single bobbled pass or a quirky bounce of the oddly-shaped football.

Such was the case in the second game of the 1984 season, when the Browns lost to the Rams, 20-17, on a spooky series of bad breaks, capped off by a looping Rams field goal in the final minutes.

Did you know?

The growing list of former Cleveland greats who have already been enshrined in the Pro Football Hall of Fame: Jim Brown, Paul Brown, Dante Lavelli, Len Ford, Otto Graham, Lou Groza, Marion Motley and Bill Willis.

> **Did you know?**
>
> *Perfecto! The 1948 Browns rolled to an unbeaten season, and then kept a perfect record by defeating San Francisco, 31-28, and then burying Buffalo 49-7 for the AAFC title game!*

A week later, the Browns lost another weird one, this time on a last-minute touchdown to the Denver Broncos.

As the season wore on, the Chiefs, Patriots and Jets also pulled off strange "miracle" finishes at the Browns' expense.

Coach Rutigliano was dumfounded at Cleveland's bad luck. At mid-season, the Browns suffered their sixth defeat in seven games. The team was still known as the "Kardiac Kids," only now they were losing in the final seconds instead of winning.

In desperation, Modell tried to stop the slide by replacing Rutigliano with Marty Schottenheimer, but Cleveland still finished a lowly 5-11. Six of the losses had been by three points or less! In nine of the games, the Browns had an opportunity to win in the last two minutes— but it was simply not to be.

COMING TOGETHER FOR THE REST OF THE EIGHTIES

"I hate losing," said Schottenheimer. "I will do everything possible to improve this team. I am committed to making the Browns the best in the league. I have a plan and the energy. We have great fans, and we have players who don't make excuses. We'll be back, you can count on that."

"I will trade all my records for a championship ring," echoed Ozzie Newsome on the eve of the 1985 season. "Great players aren't remembered just for their records. People remember them because they were winners. I

Linebacker Clay Matthews runs back another interception for the Browns.

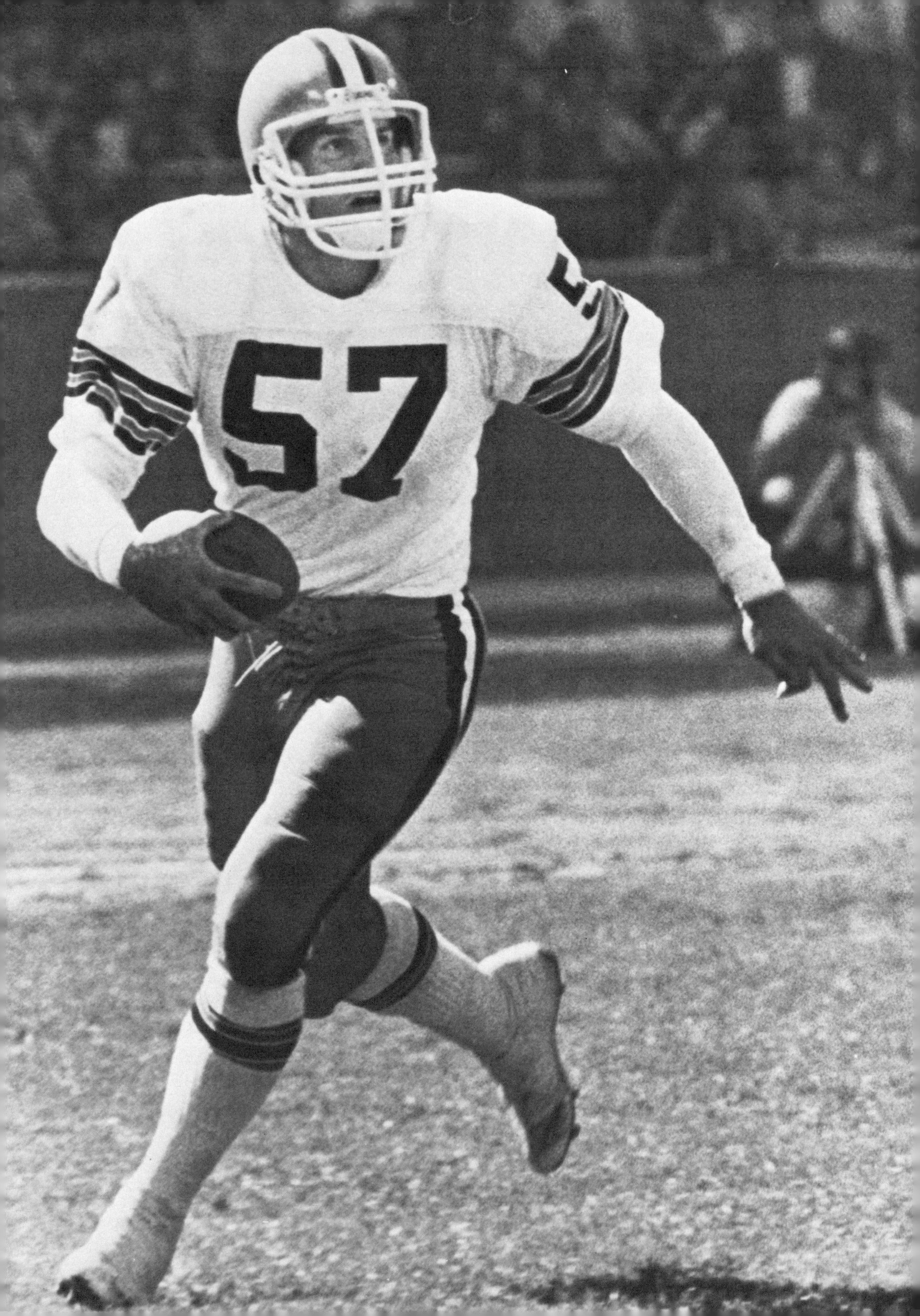
57

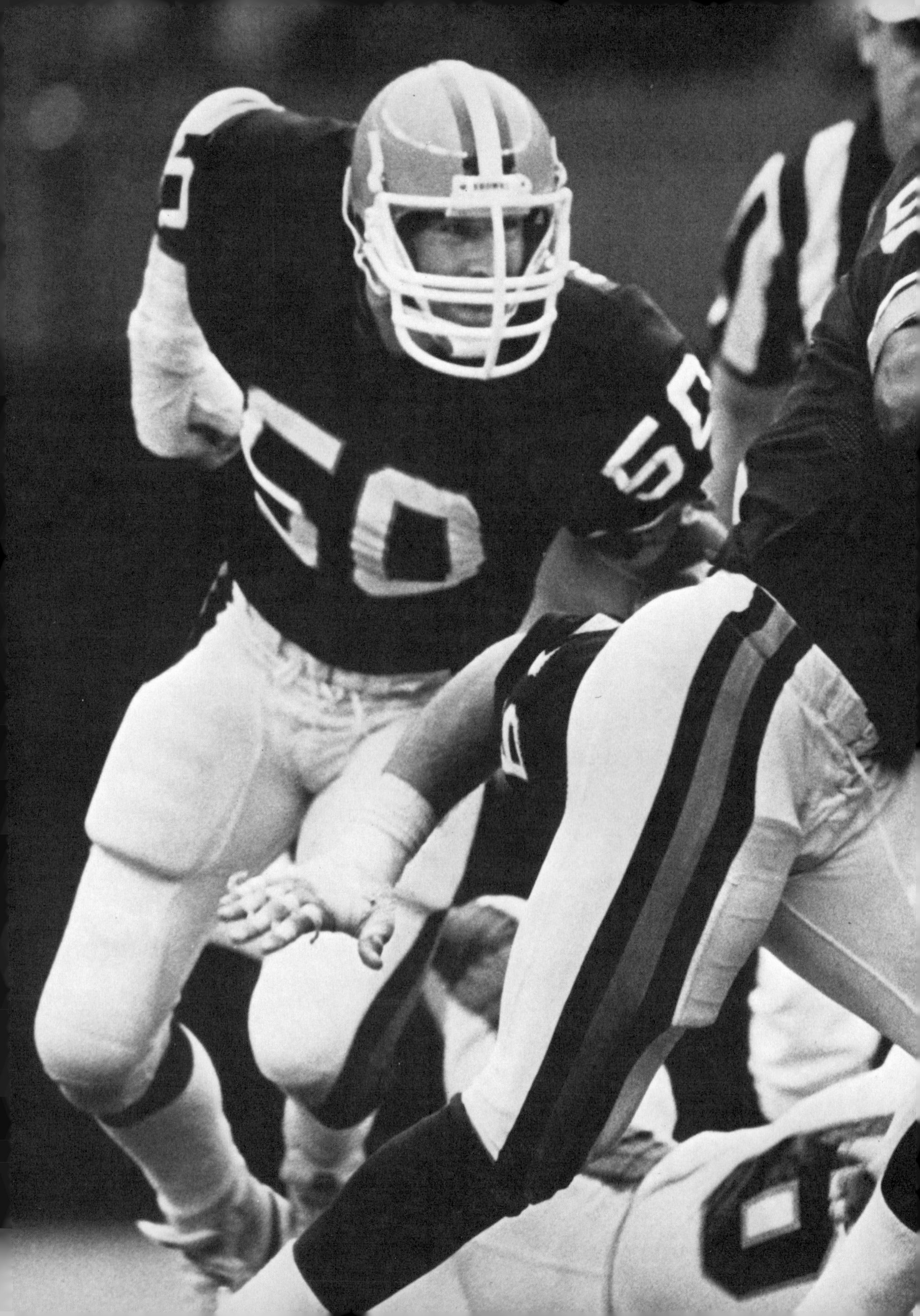

want to be remembered as a winner, and that can only happen when every player comes together in a single unified team."

Or, as the great Paul Brown once said: "Teamwork is something that every football team likes to talk about, but in Cleveland we like to think of it a sovereign tradition. Without it, you're sunk; with it, you can be invincible."

Even now, those words are resounding in the Cleveland locker room. At this moment, be assured that the mighty Cleveland Browns are pulling together for another stirring run at the NFL Championship. Watch for it!

Did you know?

Some NFL teams seem to change coaches about as often as they change lightbulbs, but not Cleveland. Head Coach Sam Rutigliano, who took the helm in 1978, became only the fifth head coach in club history!

Linebacker Tom Cousineau - a consistent leader in total tackles, solos, assists, interceptions and recovered fumbles.

NO LONGER PROPERTY OF USD 382